Round and Holy

An Homage to Donuts

Also by Chet Haase

Filthy Rich Clients
(with Romain Guy)

Flex 4 Fun

When I am King ...

When I am King ... II

Round and Holy

An Homage to Donuts

by
Chet Haase

with illustrations by
James R. Bias

First paperback printing, sometime in early 2015.
It's Winter in Northern California, which is pretty much like
every other time of the year here.

Holy crap, this is a first edition.
It must totally be worth something.

∞ . . . 1000 999 998 . . . 100 99 98 . . . 10 9 8 7 6 5 4 3 2 1

ISBN: 1507624638
ISBN-13: 978-1507624630

For the children.
Everything is for the children.

Helena, Alex, and Beatrix:
This is the book I promised to write when you
were younger. Much younger. It just took ten
years to get there, and it is a lot shorter book
than I thought it would be.

Contents

Preface

This book began life as a series of poems that I wrote on Friday mornings, as I enjoyed a donut or three at work. Or as I remembered donuts that I'd already eaten. Or as I anticipated donuts I was going to have later.

The donut has to be one of the most ridiculous, unhealthy, and sublime foods we have. It represents the essence of both everything our bodies want and everything they shouldn't have. Add the odd hole in the middle and the fun ways that donuts are decorated and you have the ultimate absurdist treat. I guess that's why donuts led to poetry, because the idea of taking the food seriously in odes and sonnets just seemed to be the next illogical step.

But mostly, it's because I love donuts. I can't think of a better way to start the day on a Friday. Or Saturday. Or Sunday. Or...

So sit back, relax, and enjoy this book. Maybe with a cup of coffee. And a donut.

Chet
January, 2015

Foreword

One of the hallmarks of a great artist is kneading
their obsessions into something more than folly.
They roll their passions into form, acknowledging
the history of their genre while cutting a wholly new
shape and boiling it into its final configuration.
Such is the work of Chet Haase in Round and
Holy. In a lifetime spent reading poetry, I have
never felt the way I do about a collection as I do
about this one.

About Haase's prosody, one can say little. He
rhymes like a baker. His rhythms are the gentle,
steady iambs of a stand-mixer left alone just a bit
too long. Yet he innovates where better poets
would have simply given up. In a pastiche on The
Night Before Christmas, he allows his rhythms to
match the particular mania of his narrator, a Poe-
ian descent into doughy, sugary madness. Rather

than acknowledge his inability to end "My Turn" on a one-beat rhyme, he craftily enjambs his last syllable, dashed and isolated like a broken last cruller tucked into the bent corner of an empty box.

Yet when he states, *"My philosophy [is] lacking and sad"* ("When There Is a Donut"), he could not be more wrong. Have greater lines about the existential crisis of being human ever been written than *"I thought I'd get a pastry but/I just got air instead"* ("There Was No Donut There")? It cries at the crux of desire and rejection, presence and absence. Yeats may have asked, *"How can we know the dancer from the dance?"* But is that really any better than:

> *Like coffee with no caffeine or*
> *A goal without a goalie,*
> *A donut with no center and*
> *No filling's just unholy*

("Tastes Great, Less Filling")? Of course it's better. But Haase tries so hard within his limited scope that we really must admire the poems in this dainty, tasty volume.

Buy this book. Like a good dozen, every bite is delicious and brings joy with every mouthful.

Dr. Mark Willhardt
Professor of Modern English and Scottish Poetry
Editor, The Routledge Who's Who in 20th-Century World Poetry

Round and Holy

An Homage to Donuts

Ode to a Donut

The problems not solved by
A donut are few,
And even those problems
Are solved by two.

Friday Donut Poem

It's not that I needed a donut today.
It's not like I'd die without it.
It's just that I know we'd be better that way;
Eat one and then you won't doubt it.

It's round and it's sticky and filled with delight,
Just gushing with goodness and fat.
Was ever there more of a wondrous sight
Than dough boiled in lard in a vat?

So stuff one down; No: two, three, or four!
There's plenty for everyone here.
We won't want them later, though there be more;
They're better with coffee than beer.

3

Halve Your Cake and Eat It, Too

He halved the donuts, citing fat
And calories and such.
It worked for me; I simply helped
Myself to twice as much.

Donut Donut Donut Donut

Donut donut donut donut
Donut donut yummy.
Donut donut donut donut
Donut donut tummy.

Ode to a Dozen Donuts

Friday donuts,
Nice and round.
Different flavors
Do abound,
Tasty whether they are big or little.

Boiled in lard in a
Great big vat,
Covered in glaze to
Make us fat.
Donuts: please go straight down to my middle.

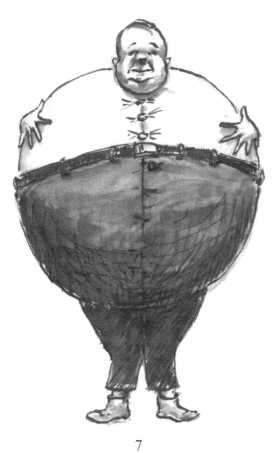

Just Donut

The week was long, the terrors real, but
Please: do not fear.
For Friday's come at last, you see:
There is a donut here.

Glazed or powdered, filled or empty,
Sprinkled or with nuts,
Donuts put love in our hearts
(The fat goes in our guts).

Donut donut donut donut
Donut donut dough;
Donut donut donut donut
Donut donut: oooohhhhh.

Donuts Are

Donuts are what we become;
Glazed and fat and round.
Each donut that's in front of me's
The best that I have found.

10

O, Donut

Donut, donut,
Round perfection;
You're my favorite
Fat confection.

Filled with cream or
Filled with naught,
You're the best thing
That I've bought.

Sitting there,
Upon my plate,
Like the other
Four I ate.

And though I'm feeling
Rather ill,
I think I'll have
Another still.

11

Rounding Factor

Light and fluffy,
Mostly round,
Worth its weight,
Pound for pound;
Donuts are the
Best I've found
For eating on a Friday.

It's not as though
They're fancy food
Or subtle; donuts
Ain't subdued.
Some might, in fact,
Just find them crude.
They're gourmet food made my way.

They're shaped like some
Majestic crown
Then deeply fried
To golden brown,
Boiled in lard
Until they're drowned,
Then dried upon a rack.

Covered with a
Sugar glaze
Or sprinkled with
A powdery haze,
Fill with goop
In many ways:
A torus heart attack.

Round and Holy

Round and holy, super gooey,
Light and fluffy, extra chewy:
Donuts are my favorite kind of food.

Have one on a Friday morn,
The day you die, the day you're born,
Eat them when you're ever in the mood.

They're perfect for a little snack;
I always keep some in my pack.
They're the food I really most adore.

14

There's nothing wrong with eating one,
Or two, or eating till they're done,
And then returning to the store for more.

So have some now, don't be shy,
There's really no good reason why
You can't just eat the whole entire box.

Have them with your morning joe
Eat them fast, eat them slow.
Fill yourself from hat down to your socks.

15

Donut: A Sonnet

Donut! Thou shouldst be living in my gut.
Eaten for my breakfast (with cup of joe)
Filled with custard, or plain, iced dough,
Yet still abide you on store shelf, but
I am Hungry! Not just somewhat,
But famished, starving, full of woe,
Blood sugar level critically low,
So weak I cannot get off my butt.

So I will hatch a devious plan,
For I must have you, many of you.
And I will get you if I e'er can;
I know exactly what I must do.
"Children," spake I, "Help your old man.
Go get some donuts, for me and you, too."

17

There Was No Donut There

When I got to work today,
There was no donut there.
This saddened me beyond belief and
Seemed a tad unfair.

I worked quite hard this week, I did,
But didn't mind the pain.
Because I knew when Friday came
I would a donut gain.

But now that there is no such treat
My joy in life is dead.
I thought I'd get a pastry but
I got just air instead.

My life was once quite filled with hope
Like donuts filled with cream,
But now there is just sadness and
A failed, pathetic dream.

18

I don't know how to carry on;
My life ahead is bleak.
I feel my soul is dying at the
Ending of this week.

But wait; what is it that I smell,
Wafting through the air?
Its lardy, sugary scent betides
That donuts now are there!

Hooray, Huzzah, and yay for me!
This week before Thanksgiving.
I have, at least today, a dozen
Reasons to keep living.

19

The Day the Donuts Broke

My Krispy Kreme was cold today;
It wasn't fresh and hot.
They sometimes come right off the line,
But these, today, did not.

I don't know why it happened thus;
Or if it was a joke
Upon this day of infamy:
The Day The Donuts Broke.

I tried one donut, then another,
Then a couple more.
None of them were warm and wet.
It made me sad and sore.

But then I found it didn't matter:
Despite the freshness date.
Boiled in fat and covered with sugar,
Each donut's worth the weight.

21

My Turn

It was my turn to go to the donut shop,
But I had no time and could not stop.
The future looked bleak and pastry-free;
I dreaded going to work.

I slowly opened my building's door
Climbed the stairs, feeling bad, more and more,
Walked past the cubes and the offices,
Feeling like such a jerk.

When what did my drooping eyes perceive,
But something I could not scarcely believe:
Two boxes of donuts were there on display;
I was saved by a kindly co-work
-er.

22

23

Tastes Great, Less Filling

My heart was filled with joy this morn
Because it's donut day.
But biting into my first choice
Didst fill me with dismay.

My solid donut was not filled
With custard or with cream
Or lemon curd or jelly; 'twas
A nightmare, not a dream.

When I get a donut with no
Hole upon its middle,
But having only dough inside it
Causes quite a riddle.

24

The pastry contract clearly states
That donuts must have holes,
Or filling otherwise or they're
Not donuts, but just rolls.

Like coffee with no caffeine or
A goal without a goalie,
A donut with no center and
No filling's just unholy.

'Twas the Night Before Donut

'Twas the night before Christmas, when all through the house
Not a donut was stirring, nor a crumb on a blouse.
The donuts were stacked by the chimney with care,
In hopes that St Nicholas would see them all there.

The children were nestled all snug in their beds,
While visions of donuts danced in their heads.
And mamma in her 'kerchief, and I with my donut,
Had just settled our brains for a big winter's donut.

When out on the lawn there arose such a clatter,
I instantly ate a big donut from the platter.
Away to the window I flew like a flash,
Then back to the donuts (no need to be rash).

A dozen fresh donuts on a gleaming white plate
Were more interesting than anything else on that date.
But what then happened to surprise all our souls,
A dozen fresh donuts, and eight donut holes.

With a donut old donut, so donut and quick.
I donut in donut, it donut St. Nick.
More donut than donuts his donuts they came
And he donut and donut, and donut by donut.

Donut, donut, donut donut.
Donut, donut, donut donut.
Donut donut, do-o-o-nut,
Donut, donut, donut, donut.

Donut donut donut donut
Donut donut donut donut
Donut donut donut donut
Donut donut donut donut.

27

Donutdonutdonutdonutdonutdonutdonutdonutdo
nutdonutdonutdonutdonutdonutdonutdonutdonut
donutdonutdonutdonutdonutdonutdonutdonutdon
utdonutdonutdonutdonutdonutdonutdonutdonutd
onutdonutdonutdonutdonutdonutdonutdonutdonu
tdonutdonutdonutdonutdonutdonutdonutdonutdo
nutdonutdonutdonutdonutdonutdonutdonutdonut
donutdonutdonutdonutdonutdonutdonutdonutdon
utdonutdonutdonut.

Donut.

29

Donut and Coffee

Donut and coffee,
Together again.
I haven't had these two
Since I don't know when.

Oh, wait - just last Friday,
Before the weekend,
I had three or four
(or five) then.

30

When There is a Donut

When there is a donut,
There is nothing wrong at all.
Life could be ruined, people could die,
Nations could crater and fall.

But if there's a donut, just one single donut,
Then everything's good as can be;
I open my mouth and suck it all in and
I am a happier me.

Some people might find me vapid,
My philosophy lacking and sad,
But when I taste the warm sugar and fat,
I figure it can't be that bad.

Everyone has their own weakness,
Their own special thing they adore.
For some it's true love or power or clothing
Or shopping all day at the store.

For others, it might be fun gadgets,
Or video games played all day long,
And who am I to judge these pursuits,
Or tell everyone that they're wrong?

But meanwhile, I just need donuts.
In fact, I'll just have that one.
(And then when I'm done with it, I'll have another;
This time a cinnamon bun).

So let all the governments fail,
And storms break the Earth's crust apart;
As long as I have my one single donut,
I'll also have joy in my heart.

ABOUT THE AUTHORS

Chet Haase lives in California, writing code for a living and comedy for fun. You can see some of his scribblings at chetchat.blogspot.com or follow him at google.com/+ChetHaase or on Twitter via @chethaase.

James R. Bias is an artist and illustrator who lives in Minneapolis, which is somewhere in the middle of the country.

18189333R00031

Made in the USA
Middletown, DE
24 February 2015